Workbook

for

Atlas of the Heart: Mapping Meaningful Connection and the Language of Human Experience

By Brené Brown

Genius Reads

Note to Readers:

This is an unofficial summary & analysis of Brené Brown's "Atlas of the Heart: Mapping Meaningful Connection and the Language of Human Experience" designed to enrich your reading experience.

Download Your Free Gift

Before you go any further, why not pick up a free gift from me for you?

Smarter Brain – a 10-part video training series to help you develop higher IQ, memory, and creativity – FAST!

www.Geniusreads.com

Table of Contents

Introduction

In *Atlas of the Heart*, Brené Brown helps us explore eighty-seven emotions and experiences that make us human. She maps for us the skills we need and creates an actionable framework so we can develop meaningful connections.

Brown has spent the last two decades understanding and studying shame, courage, vulnerability, and empathy. Extensive research into the experiences that create the person we are has helped us recognize and become familiar with courage and how to live a life from a place of courage.

She introduces this book by talking about how we become restricted to understanding and explaining what we are experiencing without having the right vocabulary. This means language is not only a tool to express ourselves. It is also what shapes our emotions.

These eighty-seven emotions and experiences that Brown discusses in *Atlas of the Heart* are a combination of emotions and thoughts that lead to emotions. They are put into groups on the basis of how they relate and compare to one another.

Brown goes on to define the four layers of emotions and experiences: biology, biography, behavior, and backstory. How emotions reflect in our bodies is biology; the role of families and communities is biography; delve into our *go-to's* is behavior; the part that gives context to a story is backstory.

She, then, with the deepest compassion and understanding, says that the anchor we are looking for is within us. Before reaching out to others and seeking meaningful connections outside, it is vital that we first connect with ourselves. The prerequisite to doing either is that we begin to understand the language of human emotion and experience.

Author's Introduction

Atlas of the Heart by Brené Brown begins with Brown sharing with us a glimpse of her childhood. She belonged to a family where people would like to accumulate things. When relatives moved houses or cities, she was entrusted with the task of packing up, something that she found both physically and emotionally exhausting. On her part, she found it immensely satisfying to lead a minimalist life.

When Brown becomes a parent, she feels pressure from some of those around her to save symbols from her kids' lives that signified growing up. She does that for a bit but eventually gives up and throws out most of the stuff. It is for this reason of not hoarding that when she comes across any box from her past with memories, putting them together would create the most accurate story of her journey through life.

The light bulb moment for Brown is when she discovers that she has been thinking about emotions – how people feel, express, and process emotions – for a long time. It is only natural then that she chose the path of deep research and exploration of the world of emotions.

Chapter 1: Places We Go When Things Are Uncertain or Too Much

This first chapter of *Atlas of the Heart* by Brené Brown begins with defining the emotions that we feel when there is either uncertainty or too much is happening – stress, overwhelm, anxiety, worry, avoidance, excitement, dread, fear, and vulnerability.

Stress

We feel stressed when something feels beyond our capacity to deal with successfully. This often comes with situations that are unpredictable, uncontrollable, and feel like an overload.

Both body and mind react to stress. The body experiences an increased heart rate and cortisol levels. Our emotional reaction, on the other hand, is governed by how we assess our ability to deal with the situation.

While stress has become part of everyday life, high levels of stress can lead to rapid aging, a decrease in immune function, less sleep, and poor health behaviors.

Overwhelm

Overwhelm is experienced when stress reaches a point where we feel that we would no longer be able to function. There is a complete giving up.

Even if others want to help us, our cognitive ability fails us to the extent that we become unsure of the next step. It's a feeling that says that what is happening around me is too much for me to process and deal with.

The cure for overwhelm is doing nothing. Non-doing helps us slowly recover from overwhelm, which renders us incapable of thinking rationally and making decisions.

Anxiety

Anxiety is a feeling that creates a lack of control. It leads to imagining worst-case scenarios and a deep sense of uncertainty. There is worry, tension, and physiological changes like increased heart rate.

Anxiety can be both a trait and a state. This means that while some of us might feel anxious as a response to certain situations, others of us can be more susceptible to feeling anxious.

Anxiety disorder is different from both these categories. It is when we excessively worry about everyday life events. It may be accompanied by fatigue, restlessness, irritability, trouble concentrating, trouble sleeping, and muscular stress.

Those who are uncomfortable with uncertainty are most likely to feel anxious. The usual coping mechanisms for anxiety are worry or avoidance – both ineffective.

Worry

Worry is not an emotion; rather, it is the thinking associated with anxiety. It is a loop of thoughts that repeats in our minds of bad things that might happen in the future.

Those who worry feel it helps them with coping, they cannot control it, and suppression of worrisome thoughts would help. All of these are incorrect.

Avoidance

Avoidance is not facing a situation but instead spending energy on how to slide past it. It can lead to a lot of damage and even more anxiety.

Often it is not fear that keeps us from doing something we want to. It is avoidance. It keeps us in our comfort zones. It can decrease vulnerability but does not decrease fear.

Excitement

Excitement is when we feel energized or enthusiastic about something. It is the same broad experience of anxiety but perceived positively, which is why it is easy to confuse one for the other.

What helps to differentiate between excitement and anxiety is taking a few moments to sit still and take a few breaths. This can help us identify the real emotion.

Dread

Dread is a response when we feel a negative event is highly likely to occur. As the time comes close to its occurrence, the intensity of dread increases.

We imagine the future negative event to unfold in the worst possible way, which is why we tend to get done with the unpleasantness of it quickly. So, in effect, the unpleasantness now could be much higher than the actual unpleasantness of the future event. But we cannot wait.

Fear

When the threat seems to be in the present moment, we respond with fear. The emotion of fear is negative, short-lived, and high alert. It is our innate response to a perceived threat that results in a fight, flight, or freeze.

Similar to anxiety, it is both a state and a trait. It is when we need to quickly respond to perceived danger. One of our biggest fears is social rejection.

Vulnerability

The emotion of vulnerability arises when there is uncertainty, risk, and emotional exposure.

While we are conditioned to believe that feeling vulnerable is a sign of weakness, it is actually what leads to courage. The prerequisite for showing courage is allowing yourself to be vulnerable.

Workbook Section

Goal:

This chapter of *Atlas of the Heart* is a map of the emotions that we experience and access when facing situations of uncertainty or too much happening. Brené Brown gives us an index of several emotions that fit into this category – stress, overwhelm, anxiety, worry, avoidance, excitement, dread, fear, and vulnerability. She talks about the importance of recognizing the emotions that we experience so we can better manage them and free ourselves from their grip.

Lesson:

Activity 1:
A great deal of this chapter has been devoted to understanding anxiety and its difference from worry, avoidance, excitement, dread, and fear. Using your experiences as a guide, take life situations and write down instances of when you thought you were anxious, but your response was one of worry, avoidance, excitement, dread, or fear.

Activity 2:
The chapter also helps us identify different ways in which we respond to real or perceived negative situations. If you had to create a map of emotions for yourself, which of these emotions do you mostly go to?

Activity 3:
This chapter teaches us a very important lesson – that of avoiding avoidance. List areas of your life where you feel you might be using the approach of avoidance as a coping mechanism.

Checklist:

Key takeaways from this chapter are:
- We respond in predictable ways to real or perceived negative situations.
- We feel stressed when something feels beyond our capacity to deal with successfully.
- Overwhelm is experienced when stress reaches a point where we feel that we can no longer function.
- Anxiety is a feeling that creates a lack of control.
- Worry is a loop of thoughts that repeats in our minds of bad things that might happen in the future.
- Avoidance is not facing a situation but instead spending energy on how to slide past it.
- Excitement is when we feel energized or enthusiastic about something.
- Dread is a response when we feel a negative event is highly likely to occur.
- When the threat seems to be in the present moment, we respond with fear.
- The emotion of vulnerability arises when there is uncertainty, risk, and emotional exposure.

Action Plan:

- Try and understand your anxiety and fear. The goal is to make friends with them so you can talk to them and explore why they are there. There is a lesson that they have for you.
- Anxiety and fear are both states and traits. Sit with yourself and try and identify which is more applicable to you. Would you define yourself as anxious and fearful, or do you experience these more as responses to certain situations?

Chapter 2: Places We Go When We Compare

The second chapter of *Atlas of the Heart* by Brené Brown is about the group of emotions we feel when we compare – comparison, admiration, reverence, envy, jealousy, resentment, schadenfreude, and freudenfreude.

Comparison

While comparison is not an emotion, it is a set of feelings that affect our relationships and sense of self-worth. We might not even be aware that we are engaging in comparison, leading to hurtful behaviors.

We use comparison to also predict future outcomes. It, therefore, kills creativity.

We compare when we want to fit in and yet want to be better. We either want to be the best or have the best. Comparison can be both upward social comparison and downward social comparison. Both have positive and negative effects – leading to thoughts of not good enough or better than. However, both lead to feelings of fear, anger, shame, and sadness.

Admiration and Reverence

Admiration is when we are inspired. It often leads to self-improvement. We don't want to become like that person; we just want to be better.

Reverence is a more intense feeling of adoration, veneration, or worship. It leads us to want a more meaningful connection with something that we consider greater than ourselves.

Envy and Jealousy

Envy is the feeling we get when another person has what we want. Jealousy is when we already have a relationship that we fear losing entirely or a valued part of.

Envy has a feeling of lack. Most feelings of envy fall into these 3 categories: attraction, competence, and wealth.

Jealousy is the fear of losing someone to another person. It is not limited to romantic relationships and can extend to parent/child relationships and with siblings, friends, and co-workers.

Resentment

Resentment is when we feel frustrated or angry or find ourselves judging or feeling 'better than.' It is envy in disguise when we perceive unfairness or injustice.

We often feel resentful when we fail to set boundaries or ask for what we need. We can also feel resentful when expectations that we cannot control let us down, for example, what other people think, feel, or how they react.

Schadenfreude

A German word, composed of two words that mean harm and joy, schadenfreude is when we experience joy or pleasure from the misfortune or suffering of someone else.

Schadenfreude indicates a lack of empathy – our emotional reaction is not in line with another person's emotional experience.

Freudenfreude

We experience freudenfreude when we enjoy another person's success.

Lack of freudenfreude can hurt a relationship. Those who are depressed can show a lack of freudenfreude.

Goal:
The second chapter of *Atlas of the Heart* is a map of the emotions that we experience and access when comparing ourselves with others. Brené Brown gives us an index of several emotions that fit into this category – comparison, admiration, reverence, envy, jealousy, resentment, schadenfreude, and freudenfreude. She talks about the importance of recognizing the emotions that we experience so we can become better versions of ourselves.

Lesson:
Activity 1: The chapter begins with Brown's recognition of how she finds herself comparing her swimming to the person in the next lane to her. Think of the things where you compare yourself with other people? **Activity 2:** Now that we know whether we are experiencing envy or jealousy, reflect if you are fearful of losing something you value to another person. If yes, what kind of conversation do you need to have with them? Also, reflect on whether you want something that someone else has. If yes, would you be okay with seeing them lose it, or is there another way? **Activity 3:** This chapter talks about triggers that elicit a shame response. Complete this sentence: "It is really important for me not to be perceived as _____."

Checklist:

Key takeaways from this chapter are:
- We compare when we want to fit in and yet want to be better.
- Admiration is when we are inspired. It often leads to self-improvement.
- Reverence is a more intense feeling of adoration, veneration, or worship.
- Envy is the feeling we get when another person has what we want.
- Jealousy is when we already have a relationship that we fear losing entirely or a valued part of.
- Resentment is when we feel frustrated or angry or find ourselves judging or feeling 'better than.'
- Schadenfreude is when we experience joy or pleasure from the misfortune or suffering of someone else.
- We experience freudenfreude when we enjoy another person's success.

Action Plan:

- When you find yourself comparing, try and become aware of what is happening and what emotions it is generating. The next time it happens, see if you can acknowledge it in your mind and respond instead by wishing the other person well.
- Think of all the things that inspire you. Write down all the ways in which you can use them to become the best version of yourself.
- When someone shares positive news about their lives, see if you can show interest and ask questions. When you share yours, and someone shows joy, see if you can express gratitude.

Chapter 3: Places We Go When Things Don't Go As Planned

The third chapter of *Atlas of the Heart* by Brené Brown is about the group of emotions we feel when things don't go as per plan – boredom, disappointment, expectations, regret, discouragement, resignation, and frustration.

Boredom

Boredom is what we experience when we want to engage in an activity that would be satisfying but is unable to do so. There is a lack of stimulation, time passes slowly, and the task seems to lack meaning or the feeling of a challenge.

Boredom can lead to feelings of irritation, frustration, restlessness, or lethargy. The good part about boredom is that it opens our minds to wandering, daydreaming, and creating.

Disappointment

Disappointment is what we experience when our expectations are not met. The bigger the unmet expectation, the bigger is the disappointment.

There are two categories of expectations:

- Unexamined and unexpressed expectations (stealth expectations): These are the most dangerous and often lead to disappointment at a high level of intensity. We have painted a picture in our minds that doesn't turn out as we had expected it to. It can bring shame, anger, and hurt while we are, at the same time, trying to conceal emotions.

- Examined and expressed expectations: This set of expectations is when we are intentional and aware and communicate them clearly. When these are not met, there is still a disappointment, especially because we allowed ourselves to be vulnerable in communicating them.

Regret

Regret arises when an outcome falls short of what we wanted or thought would happen. We hold ourselves accountable in situations that cause regret – both when we took action and when we did not.

Most regrets fall under these categories – education, career, romance, parenting, self-improvement, leisure, and acts of kindness.

Discouragement, Resignation, and Frustration

While these are all responses to things not going or not have gone as per plans, we experience discouragement when we lose confidence and enthusiasm for future effort, we experience resignation when we have lost confidence and enthusiasm for future effort, and we experience frustration when we feel something out of our control is blocking us from the desired outcome.

Workbook Section

Goal:

The third chapter of *Atlas of the Heart* is a map of the emotions that we feel when things don't go as per plan – boredom, disappointment, expectations, regret, discouragement, resignation, and frustration. She talks about the importance of recognizing the emotions that we experience so we can come out of the cycle of anger, frustration, and loss of control.

Lesson:

Activity 1:
This chapter teaches us about the importance of never losing our child-like curiosity. Do you allow yourself to be vulnerable, or do you shield yourself from the possible hurt? Journal

Activity 2:
When you find an expressed expectation not being met, rather than closing in, see if you can talk about your feelings to that person with a cue like, "I let you know how important this was to me ..."

Checklist:

Key takeaways from this chapter are:
- Boredom is what we experience when we want to engage in an activity that would be satisfying but is unable to do so.
- Disappointment is what we experience when our expectations are not met. Expectations fall under two categories: unexamined and unexpressed expectations (stealth expectations) and examined and expressed expectations.
- Regret arises when an outcome falls short of what we

wanted or thought would happen.
- We experience discouragement when we lose confidence and enthusiasm for future efforts.
- We experience resignation when we have lost confidence and enthusiasm for future efforts.
- We experience frustration when we feel something out of our control is blocking us from the desired outcome.

Action Plan:

- If you find yourself to be constantly seeking stimulation, allow yourself some time to do something repetitive or mundane. Notice what effect it has on you feeling relaxed.
- Assess if you are able to communicate your expectations to loved ones around you.
- Journal if you can use past regrets as reminders for reflection, change, and growth.

Chapter 4: Places We Go When It's Beyond Us

The fourth chapter of *Atlas of the Heart* by Brené Brown is about the group of emotions we feel when we feel something that is beyond us – awe, wonder, confusion, curiosity, interest, and surprise.

Awe and Wonder

We experience awe and wonder mostly in response to nature, art, music, spiritual experiences, or ideas.

The difference between the two is that while wonder inspires a wish for understanding, awe is more than standing back and observing.

Confusion

Confusion tells us that there is something we need to explore.

Used positively, it can motivate, lead to learning, and trigger problem-solving. Too much confusion can cause frustration, giving up, disengagement, or boredom.

Curiosity and Interest

Curiosity is when we identify a gap in our knowledge when we find something interesting and invest in exploring and learning to close that gap.

Interest is when we are open to engaging with a topic or experience.

While curiosity is both a state and a trait, interest is a state. The mind invests in interest; both mind and heart invest when there is curiosity. Interest leads to curiosity.

Surprise

Surprise is when something interrupts our current understanding or expectations. It causes us to reevaluate.

It is the emotion with the shortest life, lasting no more than a few seconds. As soon as cognition happens, we move into emotion. The emotion that we experience after is often amplified by surprise.

The difference between something perceived as a surprise and something that was unexpected is that, unlike surprise, what is 'unexpected' does not lead to emotion.

Goal:

The fourth chapter of *Atlas of the Heart* is a map of the emotions that we feel when we encounter things or situations that seem to be beyond us – awe, wonder, confusion, curiosity, interest, and surprise. She talks about the importance of recognizing these emotions that we experience so we can use them for personal growth and change.

Lesson:

Activity 1:
This chapter throws light on how we can use confusion to our advantage. The next time you find yourself dismissing new data or information, give yourself some time to think and deliberate. Can you let go of an old thinking pattern?

Checklist:

Key takeaways from this chapter are:
- Awe and wonder mostly in response to nature, art, music, spiritual experiences, or ideas. Wonder inspires a wish for understanding. Awe is standing back and observing.
- Confusion tells us that there is something we need to explore.
- Curiosity is when we identify a gap in our knowledge when we find something interesting and invest in exploring and learning to close that gap.
- Interest is when we are open to engaging with a topic or experience.
- Surprise is when something interrupts our current understanding or expectations. It causes us to reevaluate.

Action Plan:
<ul><li>The next time something inspires awe in you, reflect on how you can use it as inspiration for personal change and growth.</li><li>If there are young people in your life who you would like to see developing, see if you can inspire curiosity. You can do that by using intriguing information to first generate interest so it can lead to curiosity.</li></ul>

Chapter 5: Places We Go When Things Aren't What They Seem

The fifth chapter of *Atlas of the Heart* by Brené Brown is about the group of emotions we feel when things are not as they seem – amusement, bitterness, nostalgia, cognitive dissonance, paradox, irony, and sarcasm.

There are times when two competing emotions and contradictory thoughts co-exist. This co-existence is a reflection of our complexity.

Amusement

Amusement can be defined as "pleasurable, relaxed excitation." There is a sense of humor in amusement, along with unexpectedness, incongruity, and playfulness.

Amusement is also a short-lived emotion. One of the benefits of amusement is that it is replenishing.

Bittersweet

Bitterness is what we feel when happiness and sadness mix. Some examples are: watching children grow up, coming home from vacation, and retiring.

The sadness comes from letting go of something, while the happiness or gratitude comes from experience or what is coming next.

Bittersweet should not be confused with ambivalence, which is when we are not sure whether we are feeling happy or sad.

Nostalgia

Nostalgia is a bittersweet emotion that brings together happiness and sadness with a feeling of yearning and loss. It is a frequent, mostly positive, and contextual emotion.

It gets triggered by negative moods like loneliness and the struggle to find meaning. Our personalities and coping styles determine if we use nostalgia as a healthy or unhealthy coping strategy.

Rumination focuses on negative and pessimistic thoughts. While worry is about the future, rumination is either about the past or things about us. Rumination can lead to depression.

Reflection, on the other hand, is adaptive and healthy.

Cognitive Dissonance

We experience tension in the form of cognitive dissonance when two cognitions (ideas, attitudes, beliefs, opinions) that are inconsistent with each other co-exist. An example of cognitive dissonance is knowing that something is harmful and still doing it.

There is a whole range of mental discomfort that cognitive dissonance can produce. In order to overcome this discomfort, we use certain mechanisms like rejecting the information, reducing its importance, or avoiding it.

The greater the cognitive dissonance we feel, the more pressure we feel to reduce it.

Paradox

A paradox is when two related elements contradict. Processing a paradox means that we are able to recognize that both the elements that seem to be contradicting each other can be true.

The opposing elements of a paradox are linked to each other and complement and inform each other.

Paradox teaches us not to oversimplify and to think deeply. They cannot be resolved with logic and rationality.

Irony and Sarcasm

Both irony and sarcasm have elements of criticism and humor and are a form of communication in which what is said is different from what is implied. The difference between the two is that sarcasm is meant to ridicule, tease, or criticize.

Workbook Section

Goal:

The fifth chapter of *Atlas of the Heart* is a map of the emotions that we feel when things are not as they seem – amusement, bitterness, nostalgia, cognitive dissonance, paradox, irony, and sarcasm. There are times when two competing emotions and contradictory thoughts co-exist. This co-existence is a reflection of our complexity.

Lesson:

Activity 1:
When Brown talks about the emotion of bittersweet, she says that those who have a nuanced ability to understand emotions may more frequently experience it. Can you list some instances from your life when you have felt bittersweet?

Activity 2:
We have learned that nostalgia can be a tool for both connection and disconnection. If you find yourself resonating with the words, "I wish things were the way they used to be in the good old days," think about what is actually not spoken.

Activity 3:
Brown says that irony and sarcasm are only for playfulness and not for things we are afraid to talk about. Reflect if there are things you are disguising as humor, but that actually need clarity and honesty.

Checklist:

Key takeaways from this chapter are:
- Amusement can be defined as "pleasurable, relaxed excitation" and includes elements of humor,

- unexpectedness, incongruity, and playfulness.
- Bitterness is what we feel when happiness and sadness mix. The sadness comes from letting go of something, while the happiness/gratitude comes from the experience or what is coming next.
- Nostalgia is a bittersweet emotion that brings together happiness and sadness with a feeling of yearning and loss.
- Rumination is focusing on negative and pessimistic thoughts either about the past or things about us.
- We experience tension in the form of cognitive dissonance when two cognitions (ideas, attitudes, beliefs, opinions) that are inconsistent with each other co-exist.
- A paradox is when two related elements contradict.
- Both irony and sarcasm have elements of criticism and humor and are a form of communication in which what is said is different from what is implied.

Action Plan:

- Reflect if there is anything in your life that you ruminate about. If there is, perhaps you can journal or work with a therapist to move from a state of ruminating to reflecting.
- Cognitive dissonance, when used right, can cause us to rethink and relearn. If you identify any dissonance in you, try and stay curious, resist the path of comfort, and choose courage.
- A paradox can teach us to think in expansive ways and move towards vulnerability. Think about any paradoxes that you can work with, for example, freedom vs. responsibility.

Chapter 6: Places We Go When We Are Hurting

The sixth chapter of *Atlas of the Heart* by Brené Brown is about the group of emotions we feel when we are hurting – anguish, hopelessness, despair, sadness, and grief.

Anguish

Anguish is almost unbearable and brings together shock, incredulity, grief, and powerlessness. It not only negatively impacts our ability to breathe, think, and feel, it also causes us to physically feel the trauma.

The most debilitating thing about anguish is that we find ourselves unable to change, negotiate, or reverse what has happened.

If we experience anguish but do not find the right support to deal with it, it can be difficult for us to reengage with our lives. If we choose to tell ourselves that we are okay, we can become closed off and never open to being vulnerable.

Hope

Hope is a cognitive process. It is a way of thinking. Hope brings together goals, pathways, and agency.

We develop hope from experiences of adversity and discomfort. Our goals, pathways, and agency are tested, and we feel that change is possible. Hope is learned; we often learn hope from our parents.

Hopelessness

We feel the emotion of hopelessness when negative life events and negative thought patterns combine together, in particular, self-blame and the perception that we cannot change our circumstances.

In the case of hopelessness:

- We were not able to set realistic goals.

- Even if we do, we do not know how to achieve those goals, or we give up too soon.

- We don't believe that we are capable of achieving what we want.

Despair

We feel despair when we feel hopeless about our entire life or future. It is a result of hopelessness pervading all areas of our lives combined with extreme sadness.

While working through despair takes work and may also need the help of a therapist, we can look at Martin Seligman's research on resilience – the 3 Ps.

- Personalization: Self-blame and criticism can make us overlook external factors that contribute to the problem. We need to realize that outside factors do play a role.

- Permanence: It is thinking that the struggle will never end. What might be helpful is to think about how everything, including setbacks, is temporary.

- Pervasiveness: This is the tendency to think that the struggle has impacted every area of our lives. There is nothing good that is left.

Sadness

Sadness is a response to loss or defeat or the perception of loss or defeat. It is important for us to be familiar with sadness.

Some things to note about sadness:

- Sadness is not the same as depression.

- Sadness is not the same as grief.

- Sadness has positive aspects.

- We love sad movies because they move us from the individual to the collective.

Grief

Grief is a combination of loss, longing, and feeling lost. The more difficult it is for us to express our feelings of loss, longing, and feeling lost, the more disconnected and alone we feel.

The Center for Complicated Grief has several definitions of grief:

- Acute grief: experienced in the initial period after a loss.

- Integrated grief: experienced when we adapt to a loss and give it a place in our lives.

- Complicated grief: experienced when we are unable to adapt to the grief because of some interference.

Another term is disenfranchised grief – when what caused the grief is not publicly supported because others do not perceive it as a loss.

Workbook Section

Goal:
The sixth chapter of *Atlas of the Heart* is a map of the emotions that we feel when we are hurting – anguish, hopelessness, despair, sadness, and grief. She not only lays bare all the emotions that we experience, but she also gives us the practical tools to work through them.

Lesson:

Activity 1:
We have learned that hope involves goals, pathways, and agency. It is more a way of thinking than an emotion. Now that we have the tools, is there something in your life that you could turn from hopelessness to hope by giving it a goal, pathways, and agency?

Activity 2:
Brown talks about the importance of setting realistic goals, which are a prerequisite for hope. Can you do a reality check on your goals?

Checklist:

Key takeaways from this chapter are:
- Anguish is almost unbearable and brings together shock, incredulity, grief, and powerlessness.
- Hope is a cognitive process and a way of thinking. It brings together goals, pathways, and agency.
- We experience hopelessness when negative life events and negative thought patterns combine together, in particular, self-blame and the perception that we cannot change our circumstances.
- We feel despair when we feel hopeless about our entire

life or future.
- We can build resilience by working through the 3 Ps: personalization, permanence, and pervasiveness.
- Sadness is a response to loss or defeat or the perception of loss or defeat.
- Grief is a combination of loss, longing, and feeling lost.

Action Plan:

- Think about your childhood. How did your parents or caregivers behave during adverse circumstances? Did they show hope? Reflect if your sense of hope or hopelessness stems from there.
- Think about the things that cause you hopelessness or despair. Ask yourself – Will this affect me as much as it does now in 5 minutes? Five days? Five months? Five years?

Chapter 7: Places We Go With Others

The seventh chapter of *Atlas of the Heart* by Brené Brown is about the group of emotions we feel when we are with others – compassion, pity, empathy, sympathy, boundaries, and comparative suffering.

Compassion

Compassion is a daily practice that enables us to recognize and accept that all of us co-exist in the world, and hence we need to treat each other and ourselves with loving-kindness and take action. Compassion is not just feeling; it always comes with doing.

Pity

Pity is termed as the near enemy of compassion, which is why it is dangerous – because it is difficult to recognize.

Pity lacks the openness of compassion. It views the person who is suffering as different, separate, and distant from us. Compassion is when we can share the suffering—when we recognize it to exist within our own selves. It creates a sense of connection with the other person.

There are four elements to pity:

- a belief that the person who is suffering is inferior

- a passive reaction that does not include helping

- wanting to remain emotionally distant

- avoiding sharing in the person's suffering

Empathy

Empathy is a tool for compassion that enables us to understand what someone is experiencing and to communicate that understanding. It enables us to understand what someone is feeling but not going through the same feeling.

There are many benefits of empathy: it helps interpersonal and ethical decision-making, boosts short-term subjective well-being, strengthens relational bonds, improves our ability to understand how others see us, and enhances pro-social and altruistic behavior.

There are two elements to empathy:

- Cognitive empathy is what makes us recognize and understand another person's emotions.

- Affective empathy is when we share the experience with another. It can lead to overwhelm.

Empathy is not directly relating to the experience. Instead, it is the ability to connect with what somebody is feeling about that experience.

Sympathy

Sympathy is the near enemy of empathy. It signifies disconnection and distance. It is like saying, I feel bad for you, but where I am, these things do not happen.

Compassion fatigue is often used as a term to refer to the burnout or emotional exhaustion that caregivers can feel.

However, compassion fatigue is experienced when the focus of the caregiver is on their personal reaction to the distress of the other person rather than on the experience of the person they are caring for. This inhibits the caregiver's feeling of empathy.

Empathy Misses

1. Sympathy vs. Empathy: The difference is in the distance. Sympathy is saying I feel so sorry for you. Empathy is saying I can feel what you feel; I've been there.

2. Judgment: The person who listens to the one who is suffering feels shame for them.

3. Disappointment: The person who listens feels like they have been let down by the one who is suffering.

4. Discharging discomfort with blame: It is finding either the person who is suffering or another person to blame for the suffering.

5. Minimize / Avoid: The person listening refuses to acknowledge the intensity or the existence of the suffering.

6. Comparing / Competing: The person listening goes on to share their own story, which is much more intense.

7. Speaking truth to power: When the person listening responds to an act of standing up for yourself sounds like it shouldn't have been done or said.

8. Advice giving / Problem-solving: Rather than listening and simply being, we begin to start fixing things for the other.

Boundaries

A boundary is a line we draw between ourselves and another person. Without boundaries, there cannot be empathy and compassion.

Problems arise when what is not okay seems to be the only communication that is received. The focus on expressing and understanding what is okay can prevent unnecessary disconnection.

Comparative Suffering

Comparative suffering is the tendency to look at pain and hurt on a scale and assess others' and our pain and hurt on that scale.

Brown says that we need to understand that we need to keep perspective and understand that love, compassion, and empathy are infinite.

Workbook Section

Goal:

The seventh chapter of *Atlas of the Heart* is a map of the emotions that we feel in relation to others - compassion, pity, empathy, sympathy, boundaries, and comparative suffering. By making us deeply understand these emotions and thoughts, she helps us become more loving, compassionate, and empathetic.

Lesson:

Activity 1:
This chapter talks a lot about empathy. Here are the things to think about when you meet someone who is going through a challenging time:

Activity 1a: Take perspective. What does that concept mean for you? What is that experience like for you?

Activity 1b: Are you able to stay out of judgment and simply listen?

Activity 1c: Can you go within and feel an emotion that can help you identify and connect with what the other person might be feeling?

Activity 1d: Try and communicate your understanding of the emotion.

Activity 1e: Can you try and not push away the emotion but stay with it?

Checklist:

Key takeaways from this chapter are:

- Compassion is a daily practice that enables us to recognize and accept that all of us co-exist in the world, and hence we need to treat each other and ourselves with loving-kindness and take action.
- Pity lacks the openness of compassion. It views the person who is suffering as different, separate, and distant from us.
- Empathy is a tool for compassion that enables us to understand what someone is experiencing and to communicate that understanding. It enables us to understand what someone is feeling but not going through the same feeling.
- Sympathy is the near enemy of empathy. It signifies disconnection and distance. It is like saying, I feel bad for you, but where I am, these things do not happen.
- A boundary is a line we draw between ourselves and another person. Without boundaries, there cannot be empathy and compassion.
- Comparative suffering is the tendency to look at pain and hurt on a scale and assess others' and our pain and hurt on that scale.

Action Plan:

- Think about how you engage or connect with someone who is struggling. Is there another more effective way where you do not take their issues as your own?
- Having understood the 'empathy misses,' reflect on whether you engage in any of those.
- Journal about your boundaries – how do you define them, how do you communicate them, and how do you understand them.

Chapter 8: Places We Go When We Fall Short

The eighth chapter of *Atlas of the Heart* by Brené Brown is about the group of emotions we feel when we find ourselves falling short – shame, self-compassion, perfectionism, guilt, humiliation, and embarrassment.

Shame

In shame, the focus is on telling yourself that you are bad. You end up feeling unworthy of love, belonging, and connection and that you are flawed. It does not drive positive change.

All of us experience shame. It is universal and one of the most primitive emotions. We are all afraid to address it and express it. The less we talk about it, the more it controls us.

The cure for shame is empathy. If we open up about our perceived shameful experience and the person responds with empathy, shame disappears.

What makes shame dangerous is its lack of empathy.

The 4 elements of Shame Resilience:

- Recognizing shame when it creeps in and understanding what triggers it

- Reality-checking the messages and expectations that are driving the shame

- Reaching out to someone to speak with

- Talking about how you feel and asking for what you need

Guilt

In guilt, the focus is on the behavior rather than the self. It is like saying I have done something bad. It can lead to positive change.

We experience guilt when we fall short of our own expectations or standards. It comes with the need to do something to correct things – like apologizing or changing a behavior.

Humiliation

Humiliation is when we feel like someone else has put us down, and we do not deserve this. It leads to a feeling of being unworthy of connection and disgust with the self.

It is an intensely painful feeling of being unjustly degraded, ridiculed, or put down. It makes us feel that our identity has been demeaned or devalued.

There has emerged to be a connection between humiliation and aggression/violence.

Embarrassment

Embarrassment is fleeting and comes from feeling uncomfortable about doing something, but dismissing it is when these kinds of things happen.

It is a self-conscious discomfort that arises as a response to a minor incident in the presence of others.

Three types of situations can trigger embarrassment: committing a faux pas or social mistake, being the center of attention, or being in a sticky situation.

Self-compassion

Self-compassion is composed of self-kindness, common humanity, and mindfulness.

Self-kindness is being warm and understanding towards ourselves when we are suffering, failing, or feeling inadequate.

Common humanity is recognizing that suffering and personal inadequacy are something that everyone experiences. We are not alone.

Mindfulness is being comfortable with experiencing the feeling and not denying or suppressing them.

Perfectionism

Shame gives birth to perfectionism. It is not an effort to strive towards excellence. Rather, it is externally driven because we are always concerned about what people will think.

Perfectionism kills creativity because there is no room to make mistakes. It is the biggest barrier to mastery.

Those with high levels of perfectionism fail at meeting their own expectations, perceive themselves as always falling short of others' expectations, behave in ways that cause exclusion and rejection by others, and feel socially disconnected.

The intent of perfectionism is not self-improvement but approval and acceptance.

Perfection is self-destructive because one can never attain it. Also, it is impossible to attain a perfect perception. It is an endless cycle of feeling shame, judgment, and blame and attributing it to not being perfect.

Goal:
The eighth chapter of *Atlas of the Heart* is a map of the emotions that we feel when we find ourselves falling short – shame, self-compassion, perfectionism, guilt, humiliation, and embarrassment. She talks about the importance of recognizing one from the other so we can consciously and kindly work through them.

Lesson:
Activity 1: Using the 4 elements of Shame Resilience, recognize and assess how you are doing in being resilient to shame. **Activity 2:** This chapter teaches us the power of self-compassion. Journal a list of practical ways in which you can show more self-kindness to yourself.

Checklist:
Key takeaways from this chapter are: • In shame, the focus is on telling yourself that you are bad. You end up feeling unworthy of love, belonging, and connection and that you are flawed. • The 4 elements of Shame Resilience: recognizing shame when it creeps in and understanding what triggers it, reality-checking the messages and expectations that are driving the shame, reaching out to someone to speak with, and talking about how you feel and asking for what you need. • We experience guilt when we fall short of our own expectations or standards. It comes with the need to do

something to correct things – like apologizing or changing a behavior.

- Humiliation is when we feel like someone else has put us down, and we do not deserve this. It leads to a feeling of being unworthy of connection and disgust with the self.
- Embarrassment is fleeting and comes from feeling uncomfortable about doing something, but dismissing it is when these kinds of things happen.
- Self-compassion is composed of self-kindness, common humanity, and mindfulness.
- Shame gives birth to perfectionism. It is not an effort to strive towards excellence. Rather, it is externally driven because we are always concerned about what people will think.

Action Plan:

- We sometimes see certain things around us that make us feel or say that it is shameful. Recognize these for yourself. What are the things you think are shameful?
- Reflect on how much you lean towards perfectionism. Do you want to look perfect, live perfectly, work perfectly, and do everything perfectly? Assess whether there are any underlying feelings of shame, judgment, or blame.
- Recall some embarrassing incidents from your life that you now find funny.

Chapter 9: Places We Go When We Search For Connection

The ninth chapter of *Atlas of the Heart* by Brené Brown is about the group of emotions we feel when we search for connection – belonging, fitting in, connection, disconnection, insecurity, invisibility, and loneliness.

Belonging and Fitting in

All people inherently need love and belonging. When we do not have love and belonging, we suffer.

We need to belong as much to ourselves as to others. When there is true belonging, there is no need to change.

Our sense of belonging cannot go beyond our acceptance of ourselves. It entails that we are vulnerable, we get uncomfortable, and we are present with people as we are.

Belonging Uncertainty

We experience belonging uncertainty when we question one's social belongingness. It is high among members of marginalized groups. It is experienced as a feeling of being accepted, included, respected in, or contributing to a setting.

Connection and Disconnection

Connection is the energy that gets created between two people when they feel seen, heard, and valued, where there is an absence of judgment, and when strength and sustenance are derived from the relationship.

Those who have strong connections are happier, healthier, and more capable of handling life's stresses.

Disconnection happens when there is misunderstanding, invalidation, exclusion, humiliation, or injury. When an injured person can express the pain to the more powerful person, there can be a strengthening of connection.

It is akin to social rejection, social exclusion, and/or social isolation. The pain that this brings can be as real as physical pain.

When disconnection is not addressed, it can lead to chronic disconnection. Chronic disconnection can lead to social isolation, loneliness, and feelings of powerlessness.

Insecurity

Insecurity is a general feeling of self-doubt or lack of confidence.

There are three types of insecurity:

1. Domain-specific insecurity is when we feel insecure about a specific area or resource in life, for example, financial insecurity.

2. Relationship or interpersonal insecurity is what we feel when we find our relationship to not be supportive or trusting. This can be about one relationship or relationships in general.

3. General or personal insecurity is when we are too critical of our weaknesses.

Invisibility

Invisibility can be a painful experience, as we want to be seen, known, and loved. It is a function of disconnection and dehumanization where humanity and relevance are ignored, not acknowledged, and/or diminished in value or importance.

The different kinds of invisibility are interpersonal, group, and representational. It is a form of stigmatization.

Loneliness

Loneliness is perceived as social isolation and comes from feeling disconnected. There is an absence of meaningful social interaction.

We are genetically made to choose interdependence over independence. It is important that we do not deny our loneliness.

In order to fight loneliness, we need to have the courage to identify and acknowledge it. The next step is to find connection.

Loneliness can be dangerous. It leads to a greater risk of cardiovascular disease, dementia, depression, and anxiety.

Goal:

The ninth chapter of *Atlas of the Heart* is a map of the emotions that we feel when we search for connection – belonging, fitting in, connection, disconnection, insecurity, invisibility, and loneliness. She talks about the importance of connection and the dangers of loneliness.

Lesson:

Activity 1:
This chapter talks about disconnection and what it can lead to. Is there any disconnection that you feel in your life? See if you can describe it, talk about it, or get help.

Activity 2:
All of us tend to feel insecure. This chapter teaches us the three kinds of insecurities. Identify which ones you have and what you can do to overcome them.

Activity 3:
Are you accepting of your weaknesses? Make a list and assess.

Checklist:

Key takeaways from this chapter are:
- All people inherently need love and belonging. When we do not have love and belonging, we suffer.
- We experience belonging uncertainty when we question one's social belongingness.
- Connection is the energy that gets created between two people when they feel seen, heard, and valued, where there is an absence of judgment, and when strength and sustenance are derived from the relationship.

- Disconnection happens when there is misunderstanding, invalidation, exclusion, humiliation, or injury. When an injured person can express the pain to the more powerful person, there can be a strengthening of connection.
- Insecurity is a general feeling of self-doubt or lack of confidence.
- Invisibility is a function of disconnection and dehumanization where humanity and relevance are ignored, not acknowledged, and/or diminished in value or importance.
- Loneliness is perceived as social isolation and comes from feeling disconnected. There is an absence of meaningful social interaction.

Action Plan:

- We often try to acquire belonging by trying to fit in and hustling for approval and acceptance. Reflect on the ways in which you could be trying to be who you are not because of the need to seek approval or fit in.
- Reflect and observe if you try to protect yourself from the pain of not being able to achieve connection by keeping your thoughts and feelings to yourself rather than sharing them.
- Reflect and observe if your need for perfectionism leads you to push people away.
- Reflect if you ever deny any feelings of loneliness.

Chapter 10: Places We Go When The Heart Is Open

The tenth chapter of *Atlas of the Heart* by Brené Brown is about the group of emotions we feel when our hearts are open – love, lovelessness, heartbreak, trust, self-trust, betrayal, defensiveness, flooding, and hurt.

Love

We cultivate love when we let our most vulnerable and powerful self be seen and known, and we trust, respect, and are kind towards the connection that this creates.

It is something we nurture and grow. We can love others only as much as we love ourselves.

What hurts love is shame, blame, disrespect, betrayal, and the withholding of affection.

Heartbreak

Heartbreak is connected to love and belonging. It is more hurtful than just a painful kind of disappointment or failure.

It is what happens when love is lost. It can come from being rejected by the one we love.   We can only love when we are willing to risk heartbreak.

Trust

Trust is having the cognitive assessment that what is important to me is safe with this person.

There are seven elements to trust – boundaries (you respect my boundaries and when not sure, you ask), reliability (you do what you say you would), accountability (you accept mistakes), vault (you do not disclose my secrets), integrity (you practice your values), nonjudgment (we can talk and share without judgment), and generosity (you keep your heart open).

Self-trust is what we lose when we make mistakes. We experience a lack of self-trust when we hurt others, get hurt, feel shame, or question our worth.

Betrayal

Betrayal is a violation of trust and hence, very painful.

It can lead to high levels of anxiety, depression, anger, sadness, jealousy, decreased self-worth, embarrassment, humiliation, shame, and trauma.

It can be healed only through accountability, amends, and action. The prerequisite to that is having the courage to hear about the pain we have caused and not becoming defensive.

Defensiveness

Defensiveness is how we protect our ego and a fragile self-esteem.

When we have grounded confidence, our imperfections do not diminish our self-worth.

Flooding

Flooding is when we feel psychologically and physically overwhelmed during conflict, making a productive, problem-solving discussion impossible.

It is affected by how much stress is already present in life. We can work through it by taking time off.

Hurt

Hurt is experiencing a combination of sadness for having been emotionally wounded and fear of being vulnerable to harm. Feeling hurt is attributing someone to be doing or saying something that has caused emotional pain.

Reactions can be self-blame, retaliating, crying, lashing out, and/or seeking other relationships. Where hurt cannot be repaired, anger or sadness comes in.

Workbook Section

Goal:

The tenth chapter of *Atlas of the Heart* is a map of the emotions that we feel when our hearts are open – love, lovelessness, heartbreak, trust, self-trust, betrayal, defensiveness, flooding, and hurt. Brown takes us on a journey of trust and vulnerability so we can become comfortable with opening our hearts.

Lesson:

Activity 1:
We learn a lot about love in this chapter. Think of what love means to you and how you can put it in context with how Brown defines love.

Activity 2:
Use the BRAVING tool to think about self-trust.
- Did you respect my boundaries and communicate them?
- Were you reliable?
- Did you hold yourself accountable?
- Did you share appropriately?
- Did you act with integrity?
- Were you nonjudgmental and expressive about needing help?
- Were you generous towards yourself?

Checklist:

Key takeaways from this chapter are:
- We cultivate love when we let our most vulnerable and powerful self be seen and known and we trust, respect, and are kind towards the connection that this creates.
- Heartbreak is connected to love and belonging. It is what happens when love is lost.

- Trust is having the cognitive assessment that what is important to me is safe with this person.
- Betrayal is a violation of trust and hence, very painful.
- Defensiveness is how we protect our ego and a fragile self-esteem.
- Flooding is when we feel psychologically and physically overwhelmed during conflict, making a productive, problem-solving discussion impossible.
- Hurt is experiencing a combination of sadness for having been emotionally wounded and fear of being vulnerable to harm.

Action Plan:

- What does defensiveness look like to you? Assess if you ever try to over-justify, make excuses, minimize, blame, discredit, discount, refute, or reinterpret. Which are the situations that trigger defensiveness in you?
- Think back to when you received difficult feedback and try to remember what your body was doing, what thoughts were coming up, and what emotions you were feeling.

Chapter 11: Places We Go When Life Is Good

The eleventh chapter of *Atlas of the Heart* by Brené Brown is about the group of emotions we feel when life is good – joy, happiness, calm, contentment, gratitude, foreboding joy, relief, and tranquility.

Joy

Joy is sudden, unexpected, short-lived, and high intensity. It comes through a connection with others or with God, nature, or the universe. It fills us with freedom and abandon.

Joy is a feeling of deep spiritual connection, appreciation, and pleasure. Gratitude and joy can put us in an upward spiral.

Happiness

Happiness is longer-lived, stable, and a result of effort. There is a sense of being in control. It can be more external and circumstantial.

Happiness is feeling pleasure in context with the immediate environment or current circumstances.

Calm

Calm is keeping perspective and staying mindful while managing emotional reactivity.

Contentment

Contentment is a feeling of completeness, appreciation, and being enough. We experience contentment when our needs are satisfied.

It contributes to greater life satisfaction and well-being.

Gratitude

Gratitude is feeling and expressing appreciation. It has physical, mental, and emotional benefits and contributes to better sleep, increased creativity, decreased entitlement, decreased hostility and aggression, increased decision-making skills, and decreased blood pressure.

It allows us to be more participative in life. Since we notice the positives more, we experience a magnified pleasure.

Gratitude is a practice.

Foreboding Joy

Foreboding joy is when we feel afraid to absorb good news, wonderful moments, and joy. Joy becomes frightening, and we lose our tolerance for vulnerability.

When we push away joy, we ignore our work to build resilience, strength, and courage.

Relief

Relief is tension leaving the body. It makes us breathe more easily, feel safe, and think that the worst is over.

Sighing is an apt indication of relief. It signifies a reset.

Tranquility

Tranquility is when we do not feel pressure to do anything. It is an absence of demand. It counters mental fatigue and attention depletion.

Goal:

The eleventh chapter of *Atlas of the Heart* is a map of the emotions that we feel when life is good – joy, happiness, calm, contentment, gratitude, foreboding joy, relief, and tranquility. Brown guides us on how to use gratitude, joy, and calm to enhance our well-being.

Lesson:

Activity 1:
We learn the difference between joy and happiness. Can you write down a few examples of joy and happiness for you?

Activity 2:
Answer these questions about experiencing calm:
- Do you want to infect people with more anxiety or heal people around you with calm?
- Do you match the pace of anxiety, or do you slow things down with breath and tone?
- Do you have all the information you need to make a decision or form a response? What do you need to ask or learn?

Checklist:

Key takeaways from this chapter are:
- Joy is a feeling of deep spiritual connection, appreciation, and pleasure. Gratitude and joy can put us in an upward spiral.
- Happiness is feeling pleasure in context with the immediate environment or current circumstances.
- Calm is keeping perspective and staying mindful while managing emotional reactivity.

- Contentment is a feeling of completeness, appreciation, and being enough. We experience contentment when our needs are satisfied.
- Gratitude is feeling and expressing appreciation.
- Foreboding joy is when we feel afraid to absorb good news, wonderful moments, and joy.
- Relief is tension leaving the body. It makes us breathe more easily, feel safe, and think that the worst is over.
- Tranquility is when we do not feel pressure to do anything. It is an absence of demand.

Action Plan:

- Joy and gratitude put us in an upward spiral. Journal for 3 weeks 5 things you are grateful for and how they bring joy to your life.
- Reflect: all things considered, how satisfied are you with your life as a whole these days?
- How do you express gratitude? Do you use any of these – gratitude journals, daily gratitude meditation or prayers, creating gratitude art, or taking breaks to express gratitude?

Chapter 12: Places We Go When We Feel Wronged

The twelfth chapter of *Atlas of the Heart* by Brené Brown is about the group of emotions we feel when we feel wronged – anger, contempt, disgust, dehumanization, hate, and self-righteousness.

Anger

Anger is what we feel when something interferes with the desired outcome or when we believe that the way things should be has been violated. Someone or something else has to be blamed, and something can be done to resolve the problem.

Anger is an indicator emotion, which means that, for lack of a better word, we end up saying we are angry when what we might be experiencing is betrayal, fear, grief, injustice, regret, shame, or vulnerability.

Denying ourselves the right to be angry is denying our pain. However, maintaining anger over a long period of time is not sustainable. We need to transform it into courage, love, change, compassion, or justice.

Contempt

Contempt comes with the intention to insult and psychologically abuse your partner. Receiving contempt is shaming and belittling. It conveys disgust and superiority, especially moral, ethical, or in terms of character.

It leads to distancing, ignoring, or excluding the one who is on the receiving end of contempt. The feeling of rejection that it creates increases anxiety, depression, and sadness.

Disgust

Disgust is a more physical feeling – we want to avoid being poisoned, whether literally or figuratively. It is a feeling of aversion towards something offensive.

Its intensity can vary from mild dislike to repugnance, revolution, and intense loathing. Disgust is dehumanizing and disrespectful.

Dehumanization

Dehumanization is making the enemy into a demon, so they seem less than human and hence not worthy of being humane too.

Because the image is that of an enemy, we lose trust, get angrier and angrier, and lose our ability to listen, communicate, and empathize. Dehumanization is, therefore, a process.

Hate

Hate combines negative emotions like repulsion, disgust, anger, fear, and contempt. Lack of direct contact can strengthen hate.

The goal of hate is not just to hurt. The goal of hate is to eventually eliminate or destroy the target, either mentally by humiliating or treasuring feelings of revenge, socially by excluding or ignoring, or physically by killing or torturing. The intent is to make the one who is hated suffer.

Self-righteousness

Self-righteousness is the conviction that our beliefs and behaviors are the most correct. Such people are usually closed-minded, inflexible, intolerant of ambiguity, and less likely to consider the opinions of others.

In feeling this, we feel morally superior to others.

Workbook Section

Goal:

The twelfth chapter of *Atlas of the Heart* is a map of the emotions that we feel when we feel wronged – anger, contempt, disgust, dehumanization, hate, and self-righteousness. Brown guides us on how to process these emotions, so we do not get into the downward spiral of these negative emotions and responses.

Lesson:

Activity 1:
Think about the things that you feel make you angry. Can you identify the underlying emotions? Is there any betrayal, fear, grief, injustice, shame, or vulnerability?

Activity 2:
What are your physical responses to disgust? Think about what we learn in this chapter about disgust – do you wrinkle your nose, choke or gag, cover your mouth or nose, or recoil and back away.

Checklist:

Key takeaways from this chapter are:
- Anger is what we feel when something interferes with the desired outcome or when we believe that the way things should be has been violated.
- Contempt comes with the intention to insult and psychologically abuse your partner. Receiving contempt is shaming and belittling.
- Disgust is a more physical feeling – we want to avoid being poisoned, whether literally or figuratively. It is a feeling of aversion towards something offensive.

- Dehumanization is making the enemy into a demon, so they seem less than human and hence not worthy of being humane too.
- Hate combines negative emotions like repulsion, disgust, anger, fear, and contempt. The goal of hate is to eventually eliminate or destroy the target, either mentally by humiliating or treasuring feelings of revenge, socially by excluding or ignoring, or physically by killing or torturing.
- Self-righteousness is the conviction that our beliefs and behaviors are the most correct.

Action Plan:

- Language matters. When you come across a language that can strip people of their dignity and humanity, try and become aware of how dehumanization is working. See if you can call it out.
- Identify any beliefs or convictions that you might be holding that border towards self-righteousness.

Chapter 13: Places We Go To Self-Assess

The thirteenth chapter of *Atlas of the Heart* by Brené Brown is about the group of emotions we feel when we self-assess – pride, hubris, and humility.

Pride

Pride is when we feel pleasure or celebratory because of our accomplishments or efforts.

Authentic pride is when we feel accomplished, triumphant, and confident. However, pride can also be used in a negative context, something like – pride got in the way. What can interfere is hubris, fear, shame, or defensiveness.

Hubris

Hubris is an inflated assessment of our innate abilities. It comes from the need for dominance rather than accomplishment. The need for dominance does not require social acceptance.

Higher hubris correlates with lower self-esteem and higher narcissism and shame proneness. Those with high hubris are more likely to experience chronic anxiety, engage in aggression and hostility, and struggle with intimate relationships and social support.

Narcissism is the shame-based fear that we are ordinary.

Humility

Humility is being grounded. It is more genuine and powerful compared to hubris.

Humility is the openness to learn while maintaining a balanced and accurate assessment of our strengths, imperfections, and opportunities for growth.

Modesty is different from humility. Modesty is when you downplay your accomplishments.

Intellectual humility is when we are open to hearing other points of view and willing to adjust our beliefs on receiving new information.

Workbook Section

Goal:
The twelfth chapter of *Atlas of the Heart* is a map of the emotions that we feel when we feel wronged – anger, contempt, disgust, dehumanization, hate, and self-righteousness. Brown guides us on how to process these emotions, so we do not get into the downward spiral of these negative emotions and responses.

Lesson:
Activity 1: Think about what inspires authentic pride in you. Make a list of all the things that make you feel proud of your accomplishments and efforts. **Activity 2:** Observe if you can identify patterns of dominance display – the head has a downward rather than an upward tilt, the stance is widened, and there is less smiling.

Checklist:
Key takeaways from this chapter are: • Anger is what we feel when something interferes with the desired outcome or when we believe that the way things should be has been violated. • Contempt comes with the intention to insult and psychologically abuse your partner. Receiving contempt is shaming and belittling. • Disgust is a more physical feeling – we want to avoid being poisoned, whether literally or figuratively. It is a feeling of aversion towards something offensive. • Dehumanization is making the enemy into a demon, so

they seem less than human and hence not worthy of being humane too.

- Hate combines negative emotions like repulsion, disgust, anger, fear, and contempt. The goal of hate is to eventually eliminate or destroy the target, either mentally by humiliating or treasuring feelings of revenge, socially by excluding or ignoring, or physically by killing or torturing.
- Self-righteousness is the conviction that our beliefs and behaviors are the most correct.

Action Plan:

- Humility can be a source of strength. Think about how you respond to new information and how you assess yourself in terms of your strengths, imperfections, and opportunities for growth.

Thank You!

Hope you've enjoyed your reading experience.

We here at Genius Reads will always strive to deliver to you the highest quality guides.

So, I'd like to thank you for supporting us and reading until the very end.

Before you go, would you mind leaving us a review on Amazon?

It will mean a lot to us and support us in creating high-quality guides for you in the future.

Warmly yours,

The **Genius Reads** Team

91740496R00046